C

Contents

Foreword

Regardless of the eons I've spent spinning out television games, I never fail to be amazed at how certain of them 'travel' so effectively through different nations and cultures.

I should have been least surprised to discover than the most universal of all notions – that children are a delight – should have caught on everywhere in the world. And that's indeed the case with 'Child's Play', which not only made it on American television but has found success in Australia, England, France and a growing number of other foreign lands.

When we first tried the idea in the US, we were amazed at the seemingly innate ability of most children to *sense* the meaning of a word, and then be able to articulate that meaning. If you've ever set out yourself to try to define a word ('love', 'boredom', 'slavery', 'jealousy') you'll realize how difficult a task it is for non-lexicographers. Yet children with no experience whatsoever in defining anything take to it like a fish to water.

What a child frequently does, by facial expression and body language, is to project the *emotional* sense of the word. Of course, children do sometimes go wide of the mark and bravely take a shot at defining a word quite outside the periphery of their knowledge. They'll charge forward with a meaning that's quite hopelessly incorrect. But even then there's a charm and a warm delight in watching children *try*.

As we become adult we quickly learn to be cautious, and to protect ourselves with the armour of carefully chosen words. A child has no such armour. And it's that sweet openness, that lack of guile, that innocence, that makes the rest of us feel good about children – and ourselves.

MARK GOODSON
April 1985

Introduction

When Alan Boyd of London Weekend Television first asked me to present 'Child's Play', I hesitated. My instincts told me that it would be one of those twee and embarrassing programmes, filled with cute and knowing kids. My instincts, as usual, were wrong.

'Child's Play' was an immediate success, without any of the afore-mentioned horrors. What viewers were offered was a fresh, uncluttered view of the world, sometimes slightly off-centre, but always entertaining. It reassured us all to see that innocence and optimism were still flourishing in the children of the late twentieth century.

The format of the show was simple. Children aged between five and eleven were asked to define a selection of everyday words, without actually uttering the words in question. Sometimes the temptation was too strong, at which point the 'oops' factor was brought into play, masking the mouth and bleeping out the offending sound. Teams of grown-ups then had to guess the word being defined. Result – a mixture of hilarity and poignancy. The adults who took part, mostly well-known faces, cheerfully accepted second billing; the children were the stars.

'Child's Play' brought instant fame to several young contributors – but a short-lived fame. Over the months, those chubby, gap-toothed faces lengthened and matured before our very eyes. They became veterans and, sad though we were to see them go, it was pleasing to know there were a lot more where they came from.

A tribute is due to the camera crews who waited patiently at the schools all over Britain to capture the precious pearls, puns and flights of fancy.

This collection, culled from the first two series, comes direct to you without the facial contortions and acrobatics that were often involved, but still manages to be funny and enlightening, and brings back happy memories for me. It's a nice thought too, that it should help improve the quality of other young lives. The royalties from every copy sold will go to the Save the Children Fund.

One final self-indulgence. As we're celebrating the mysterious workings of the young mind, let me recount the time I took one of my six children, Jane (then aged about seven) for a stroll through the local graveyard. We stopped at a tombstone, the inscription on which finished with the words 'well done'. 'Daddy,' said Jane, 'does that mean he was cremated?'

MICHAEL ASPEL
April 1985

Body Beautiful

Brain

Some people would think it's white, and it's got a circle at the bottom, then lots of arches over the top, and when you're thinking of questions it always tells you the answer . . . and it doesn't control any part of you, but it's very handy at times.

David Mance, 7

It's like a form of tubes put together, and you have to use it for a lot of things . . . nearly everyone should have one.

Sherry Ralph, 8

Figure

People have them, animals have them. On people they're white or light pink. Women have the best ones.

Gregory Heard, 11

Waist

It's a kind of big joint that allows you to twist around and touch your toes and do other sort of gymnastic exercises. It is a very useful part of the body, and without it we would be totally flimsy and helpless.

Anthony Peacock, 9

They're on your body and they're curvy, shaped like a peanut, shaped like a peanut shell. Everybody's got them and you can waggle them a bit.

Geoffrey Denyer, 7

They're sort of in the middle of your body and a lot of people don't know what they're for, but they're to hold your trousers up and lots of people wiggle them. They look really silly.

Tiffany Legge, 11

Holly Aiken

Skin

I've got some and it keeps me warm and it's hard.
And my dad's got some but it's medium and my
mum's got some but it's soft.

Paul White, 8

It's better than glue to keep your body together. When
you're older you'll have more of it 'cause you will be
bigger and it will be bigger with you.

Beverley Croft, 8

Toe

A toe is a kind of thing that's on your foot and it is
smelly and it goes into your shoe sometimes with
your foot.

Marlon Truscott, 5

Muscles

Big Daddy's got a lot, Des O'Connor hasn't got any,
boys have got them. There's a girl in my class whose
name is Lisa Armstrong and people call her Armstrong
'cause she's got a lot of these.

Gayle Swanson, 8

Skeleton

If you see one without its covering on it's white . . . I think it's white before it goes mouldy. If you didn't have one you wouldn't be able to do gymnastics or swimming because everything would just go flop.

Nicola Smith, 10

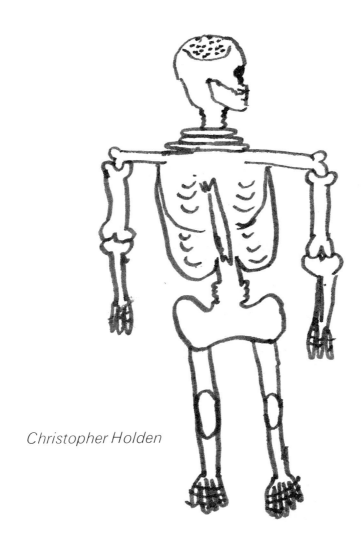

Christopher Holden

Body

I think inside it, it would look all gooey and it would
be red, white and pink and dark red and all colours
like that . . . there would be big lumps of flesh and all
long stringy things and things like that.

Gregory Heard, 11

There isn't anybody that hasn't
got one. Well, it's more or less all
of yourself . . . apart from your
hair.

David Mance, 7

Fat

Nicola Solloway

16

Baby

It comes out of your Mummy, and they eat sort of sausages on a string.

David Mance, 7

Peter Jamieson

Adult

She can be quite young, or about eighty-three or something. It's when you're thirty-two or twenty-one and you don't go to school unless you're a teacher . . . and then you go to night school. And you kind of go to work and do jobs like being a nurse and stuff what we can't do. That's it.

Debbie Newburn, 11

Middle-aged

Roger Moore is it, Harrison Ford is it, the Prime
Minister is it. The Queen's it and my mum and dad
are it. Most actors and actresses are it.

Alice and Luke Hargreaves, 6 and 10

Sometimes your hair goes a bit grey, and you get fatter and you
sometimes lose a bit of your hair and you get really older and you think
you're getting really old but you're not very old, you just think you're
old because your hair's going grey and you're getting fat and your hair's
falling out.

Stuart Butler, 9

It means that you're not exactly old but that you're
not exactly young and it's in between old and young,
and it can be fun being like it but I don't know
because I'm not middle-aged.

Veronica Miller, 7

Mother-in-law

An old lady that used to be your
old mum . . . and she can knit and
she can sew.

James Street, 5

Old

Animals can be it but ants can't 'cause they might get stepped on. Tortoises can be it 'cause they get very 'it' and the trees can get 'it' 'cause they creak about in the air and you can hear them.

Mark Banwell, 10

You can cook when you're it, and you can have a house and a car and you can tell children what to do.

Tom Groves, 5

Nicola Solloway

Granny

I've got one of these and we go down the British Legion every Saturday, and she has a pint of Guinness and I have a lemonade, we play space invaders and I don't let her win. If she loses she usually jumps up and down in a gip.

Selwyn Strick, 11

Well, we've got one and she's kind. She lives in a flat, and she comes to our house on Saturdays. She always spoils us because my mummy doesn't like it really.

Victoria and Alexandra Groom, 5

Teresa Jane Bland

Food,
Glorious Food

Porridge

It's a kind of whitey lumpy colour,
I certainly don't like it. My dad
loves it and he might marry it.

Murray and Mark Steele, 5 and 8

Liver

It's dark red and it's sort of soft, and it's easy to chew when you put it in your mouth. Some people don't like it very much, but some do. And people who don't like it don't eat it because they don't fancy it. And a girl called Jennifer Watson who left our school in September, she didn't like it either.

Judith Ballantyne, 8

It's purple and very slimy, and when you cut it open
it's all full of tubes. And you can fry it with onions
and sometimes bean sprouts . . . and when it's cooked
it looks all warty and everything.

Andrew Kelso, 9

I think sometimes you eat it and sometimes it's brown
and most of the time it's from cows. It's sometimes
part of your body.

Jamie Matthews, 6

Sausage

Neil Smith

Well, they're round things, they're brown, and they've got sort of stuff in the middle, and you can eat them. They've got crispy stuff around the meat.

Neil Smith, 7

I can eat about two or three or four or five or six or . . . one or two . . . I can eat. They're all in a row, and sometimes you get them again and again and again and again.

Mark Badham, 5

Mashed potato

It's got lots of lumps on it but it's very soft. You can have it at any school if you have school dinners. You would have it cooked mostly unless you had a very funny appetite.

David Mance, 7

Gobble

It's a horrible noise . . . it's like a waitress pushing a trolley over a cattle grid. No, it's not a waitress 'cause a waitress would fall in.

Tiffany Legge, 11

Well, it's when you eat fast. My sister does it when she's eating crisps, and my teacher does it. He eats very fast and very noisily. My dad sometimes does it as well.

Susan Keirl, 11

Vitamins

Well, I have them for breakfast, you can't see them
and you get them in Rice Crispies and Corn Flakes.
You can't really taste them.

Andrew Ebsary, 10

They are very good for you and they are recommended
by doctors and other people, and if you take these
they will give you a very healthy life and lots of people
want to lead very healthy lives.

Anthony Peacock, 9

You get them in pharmacies and chemists, and you
get them in food like meat, potatoes and greens and
they're very good for colds and the 'flu.

Llewellyn Morgan, 9

Tanya Jackson

Rotten

It's smelly. If people are like it they're unkind to people and they shout and boss people about, it's smelly and things like old apple cores can smell when they're in dustbins.

Josephine Carnegie, 8

Josephine Carnegie

Beer

James Tovell

Well, Dad makes it at this tube . . . and there's this bottle with the beer in it and there's this tube, and you blow down the tube, or rather you suck down it, and you quickly stick it in, and if the beer comes down you know it's ready, but if it doesn't come down you blow it in again and put it back in and you keep on doing it if it doesn't work until it does do it. And when you've done that you can put it in a bottle, replace the cork, and it's ready to drink after a shake or two, I think.

Veronica Miller, 7

Well, it's a drink, and it makes your stomach go out, and you get very ill, and you can go to the toilet a lot.

Mark Cavanagh, 11

It's a drink that tastes sort of like polluted water, and mostly men drink it, but occasionally you can get women that drink this as well.

Ewan Jenkins, 10

Hangover

It's when you're sort of like ill or something and you don't feel fit to walk, you just want to lie in bed and everything, you don't want to get up, and sometimes when you've had a very big lunch or something, that's what you get.

Elan Diamond, 9

This is when somebody if you see them, they'll have red eyes and their face will go up and they'll stagger and shiver and walk sidewards and I don't think they should drive like that, they do it because it makes them feel cheery. That's all I can say about it.

Aamir Aslam, 10

You've got a headache and you've got bags under your eyes and you're awful lazy and you're tired and you've got pains everywhere and your head's spinning and the best way to cure it is to have a cup of black coffee.

Anne Christie, 9

Snack

Well, I have these at about ten o'clock and perhaps even eleven, and I have one at twelve o'clock, and then I have one at about three o'clock and sometimes I even have one at five or six o'clock . . . and then I usually have one at about half past eight and quite a lot of people have them, and I like them.

Ieaun Hall, 9

Jennifer Foster

Pickles

Justin Barrett

The Land of Make-Believe

Alien

You can get them green red and purple . . . they have
spots. . . . They speak in a different language. Some
have an eye in the middle of their face, some of them
have noses. Some are nice and some are nasty – most
of them are nasty.

Lucy Cropper, 6

Well, they've got tentacles, probably lots and lots of them . . . and they
come here 'cause of the climate. I think it might be because it's colder
where they are than it is here, so they come here to get the warmth. Or
perhaps it's warmer where they are and they come here to get the cold.

Andrew Heals, 10

Someone who comes from outer space. . . . They live
on the Moon and on Mars. I've seen one, but I don't
know what they look like.

James Street, 5

Simon Claridge

Dragon

They're not pets and they could be rather vicious.
They just eat normal foods, I think. Some might be
vicious and some might not be vicious, it depends.
There might be baby ones, and mummy ones, and
daddy ones – maybe they all live like we do in
another world or somewhere.

Claire Sutherland, 8

You usually find them in caves, and you don't find
them in shops and arcades and things like that, and
you couldn't just take them out for a walk, they're
very fierce. And when they breathe fire out of their
mouths, you can usually make toast like that, and you
get them in the woods and in Loch Ness and in
places like that.

Justine McKellar, 9

Christopher Holden

Fairy

They're all over the world, and once Alex saw one in Australia. You can have them in France because they left me some francs. They wear white dresses and sometimes they sit around in Heaven talking to each other.

Nicholas Maloney, 8

I think they eat baked beans.

James Sutherland, 5

I don't know where they are, we don't know where they live because you can't see them. You never ever see them in the daytime because you might frighten them.

Emma Pitman, 5

Fairy story

It's a kind of story, but it's never true . . . and if someone thinks it's true, I shall call them a dumbdolly.

Marlon Truscott, 5

Martine Frodsham

Ghost

People think they see them at night but they see owls and things. They see some things that come out at night but they think they're ghosts sometimes, but they think they're them sometimes, but they're owls and things.

Robert Rough, 6

It wears a cloak, it eats spaghetti ... it flies. They have no legs.

Nigel Canavan, 7

Genevieve Ryan

Dream

Justin Barrett

Robot

Well, they haven't got a beard, they haven't got hair, they're mainly shaped squares with square heads and square bodies. They sort of talk in a strange language – I don't know the language. That's it, I don't know any more about them.

Paul Sewell, 7

It's made out of metal and they haven't got a heart and it doesn't laugh when you tell it a joke. Instead of having bones inside it, it has all wires. There's not enough room for a heart and it says, 'You are a prisoner'.

Patrick Mold, 6

A597

1 2 3 4 5 6 7
8 9 10

A B C D E F G H I J K
L M N O P Q R S T U
V W X Y Z

cancel

Robert Thornton

Paradise

This is like a place where I don't think no one's ever come back from. When you go up there, you don't come back again, and you can take it easy, you don't have to go to work or school. Well, you'd be past school age anyway probably when you went.

Nicola Smith, 10

It's the best thing that ever happened to you in your life. You really think it's fantastic and it's really nice. For me, it would be free admission into Stirling swimming baths.

Victoria Wilson, 9

It's not in Scotland and it must be a place that's quite hot. It wouldn't be easy to get there – no plane or boat or car could ever get there.

Christopher Wishart, 8

Lisa Marsh

Heaven

I think from looking at it from somewhere, it would be all red and they could just see it in a sort of darkish brown in all the things in the background. I think there will be churches and square things but they would be sharp, but they would just look as if they were sort of boxes. Well, another thought, inside I think there would be a sort of cave with all little paths leading to it and all the people would be laying on the floor and mumbling and groaning and moaning.

Victoria Baker, 9

I think they would just sit and pray all day and they wear long white robes with gold belts, and Jesus sandals.

Layla Botton, 9

It's a place where you go up this dark tunnel and there are these gigantic doors at the end, they're plated with gold and there's this great big light and you have to close your eyes.

Lee Cowley, 6

Hell

It's a place, it's cold; you're like a slave, you carry and fetch all day. And you only get a bit of food. It's damp.

Layla Botton, 9

Some people think that the person down there puts you in a cooking pot and boils you with custard.

David Maton, 8

It's a very bad place to go 'cause you get whipped. You can get starved to death, and sometimes you can get eaten by a monster or something.

Fiona Ritchie, 8

Monster

Matthew Thomas

Going Places

Abroad

They're not like us . . . we eat mince and potatoes.
They might not eat mince and potatoes, they might
eat snails and frog's legs. Sometimes, their water isn't
as clean as it is here.

Judith Ballantyne, 8

Sometimes you go by aeroplane, boat . . . or car . . .
like if you were going to Wales where my Grandma
lives.

Christopher Jones, 6

Africa

Justin Barrett

Adventure

I've got lots of books about it and it's very exciting. Sometimes though, when I read these books about them and if I stop off in a very exciting place, I get all nervous and worried so I have to read on until I come to a nice part – of the book, that is, and there are lots of books about it. I like the Famous Five.

Veronica Miller, 7

Russia

I think they've got the jungles up there, well, somewhere, anyway. And it's one of those foreign countries, and of course you know they don't talk English.

Ian Evenden, 5

America

Douglas Reed

Occupational Hazards

Important

Well, here are some of the people on television who are it . . . the Prime Minister . . . Cliff Richard . . . Mickey Mouse . . . Bugs Bunny . . . Donald Duck . . . Road Runner.

Veronica Miller, 8

Lots of things are this, like making sure you've got your crisp money for school and that you clean your teeth every morning just in case they turn yellow or green and the boys won't want to kiss you.

Sandra Evans, 9

Julius Caesar

Well, he wears a hat which is mainly made of silver and it's got red hairs all across the top of it from the front of the hat down to the back. And he was a soldier and he probably eats more fruit than what we do, maybe!

Sherry Ralph, 8

He lived in a big house in Rome and he fought lots of battles and he conquered England and he ruled England, and most of the time when he wasn't fighting battles he would be in a house drinking wine and eating and being served on and being in bed and places like that and lazing around.

Lyndon Nicholas, 10

She's from a show and she's got blonde hair. I think that's all I know about her.

David Mance, 7

King

Well, they don't shake hands like we all do, they only shake with their fingertips, otherwise there's a possibility their hand could go flat. I don't think they should do judo or karate or go into battles because they might get killed.

Simon Catley, 8

Simon Catley

Prince Charles

I like his face and I like his leg, and I like the way that he dresses up when he's going out somewhere. He's just good looking, I don't know why but he's just good looking.

Sarah Hay, 6

If he ever came to my house, we'd have to move beds 'cause there wouldn't be enough room. I'd have to sleep in my brother's room and he'd sleep in my room. And we'd get lots of posh food in like cakes and sandwiches.

Naomi Packer, 8

Malcolm Hogg

Princess

She sits in a big chair, she's got a big long bed and the castle's made of stones and it's got a big moat round it and they've got some crocodiles in it and they've got a big bridge what's made of wood what closes up onto the castle so the baddies couldn't get in.

Eamon Urtone, 5

Tracey Brown

Diana, Princess of Wales

If she came round to my house I'd be very honoured
. . . and I'd faint. I would show her my computer, but
she may not be up to that sort of thing.

Christopher Dickson, 8

Prime Minister

Well, to be one of these you have
to be quite good at maths and
things like that.

Amelie Chevalier, 9

They have somebody who like
puts things like electric and gas
up and down, and things like that.

Lisa Catterall, 8

Helen Bushby

Clown

Claire Warren

Genius

My brother isn't one but my dad is 'cause he helps Mum, like doing the washing up and helps put the nappy on the baby. Sometimes he takes me to gymnastics. He gets the milk.

Sarah Foster, 7

Not many people like him because he goes round answering all these questions and things like that, and all the people don't know the answers. And he's not very good at sport. They're normally just good at questions and work and they're always getting house points for their team and their team always wins, and that's just because he's brainy.

Lyndon Nicholas, 10

You can get computer ones, some mathematic ones, all different subject ones. I don't know any, I'm certainly not one.

Gregory Heard, 11

Secretary

Well, my daddy, he's got a secretary and he likes her very much . . . her name's Tracey and she gave us two bunny rabbits but one of them ran away . . . at Christmas she has to make him all his cakes.

Caroline Stanbridge, 10

An invention

Christopher Holden

Psychiatrist

They're people you go to see when you're in love or you've just been divorced or you've got problems like those. Maybe you've been stuck underground somewhere, and you can go and see them every two weeks for a little while and see if they can help you overcome these problems.

Ewan Jenkins, 10

He's higher than a doctor, in a different sort of way. It can be a man or a woman. He sort of sees to your brain . . . and the ones that I've seen always wear glasses.

Carl Spencer and Richard Vaughan, 9

You can have psychiatrists for different things, like ears and your eyes . . . feet, nose, tonsils, your mouth if you've got ulcers on your tooth. If they think something's wrong with your eyes, they tell you.

Aaron Andrews and Theresa Bland, 9

Monk

They usually live with lots of others of their kind. They're rather like human beings and they're good at karate.

Alice and Luke Hargreaves, 6 and 10

There was one up in Scotland who lived with Columbo.

Iain Russell, 8

Douglas Reed

Ballet

Dainty men do it . . . it's quite quiet and they stretch about.

Michael Reynolds, 10

You shouldn't look at them in case they go wrong.

Rebecca Strawbridge, 8

My cousin goes to it. She's a girl, and I've got a cousin who's a boy who goes to Cubs.

Llewellyn Morgan, 9

Sally-Ann Hardwidge

Slave

They're different from other people because they
don't have the same clothes, they have rags and they
don't have nice food like we do and they do very hard
work, they don't go to sleep, they work all night and
they get paid very little, one pound each day.

Llewellyn Morgan, 9

If I had one I'd ask it to bring me breakfast in bed and
a cup of tea or something in the morning so that I
wouldn't have to do it myself.

Lisa Wills, 9

Lisa Wills

Caveman

They lived with the dinosaurs and they ate raw meat and their teeth always fell out 'cause they didn't invent toothbrushes, and that's all.

Beverley Croft, 8

Terry Wogan

He's a TV star and he's got blond hair. He's famous but I can't remember what he's famous for. He's about four foot something . . . five foot.

Robert Thornton, 8

He's got black hair and he always wears a grey suit. He's medium height, he's medium thickness.

Alice and Luke Hargreaves, 6 and 10

I think he's a footballer or something . . . something to do with football.

Sarah Foster, 7

Lisa Browning

Supermen

Hero

It's someone when they've done something good, and sometimes they go to the queen, and they put a sword on each side of their shoulders. Once I saw a film and they done something brave and he didn't kneel down properly and they put one on one shoulder and chopped his head off.

Brett Seagrave, 6

It's somebody who does good things, like Superman or Mighty Mouse.

Paul Sewell, 7

Neil Smith

God

Aron Andrews

Brave

I was it once, and I was stuck on a shed roof at
Diane's house. They tried to make steps with bricks
but it wouldn't work so in the end I had to jump off
the top.

David Mance, 7

In 1942, a Wellington bomber . . . its port engine
caught fire so the co-pilot of the plane got out from
the window, went onto the wing and smothered the
flames, so he was being this.

Colin Armes, 10

Dangerous

Well, if you get a knife, that's it, and if you get a sword and stab
somebody, that's it, and if you fall down a rock and you can't get up,
that's it. If you fall down a mountain, that's it, and if you get knocked
over, that's it, and if you get a knife and cut yourself, that's it, and if you
get a very sharp axe and chop your finger off, that's it.

Patrick McElroy, 6

James Bond

David Jones

Happy Days

Relax

Well, it's something where you either sit down sort of lying down or you lie down completely and you don't go to sleep or anything like that, but if you're in this sort of lying-sitting position, you put your feet up. There's no need to do that if you're in the lying down position 'cause your feet are already up.

Veronica Miller, 7

When I lie down and read a book, that's when I do it to myself. I don't often read books to myself and when I relax I lie on my bed and play with my space invaders game, it's called a missile invader and it drives my mother crazy when I play it.

Llewellyn Morgan, 9

Polite

The Queen is this, and if she wasn't this, the chauffeurs wouldn't take her and she would have to travel by London Transport. And if the Queen wasn't it, all the people would say, 'We don't want to be ruled over by this Queen, let's go independent.'

Simon Catley, 8

It's when you use your manners, and say if you went to a house and you eat all your food, if you stayed for tea you've got to say please and thank you, and you mustn't throw food around a table when you're eating, and you've got to close your mouth when you eat.

Brett Seagrave, 7

Comfortable

Well, it's very nice, and most often when you kneel
it's very 'it'. And cushions are very it as well, and it's a
very nice word to think of because it's very usually
warm and soft whatever it is that's it . . . and of
course, no one can say that beds aren't it.

Veronica Miller, 7

I'm this in my trousers, my jumper and my trainers . . .
and I'm this on a train but not on a bus. I don't like it
on a bus 'cause it's got spikes on the seats, but I like
it on a train 'cause it's soft.

Tanya Jackson, 10

Philip Shuttleworth

Cuddle

You see people doing this at a football match when somebody's scored a goal – they do this to each other and they jump up on top of each other. And if you've fallen out with somebody, I don't think they'd do this to you.

Anne Christie, 9

Well, you sometimes might fall over or don't feel very well and you might want one then sometimes. I just want one 'cause I feel like it.

Sally-Ann Hardwidge, 6

Well, mums and dads do it sometimes . . . and when your fat uncle does it, he squashes you to death nearly.

Disma Hills, 10

My brother Stephen does it to me sometimes, and well, he likes it really, and I like it. We all like it really. Also, when I get upset my mum says, 'Come and have a cuddle.'

Sharon Tiara, 9

Fun

For Superman it would be flying
upside down catching robbers. It
wouldn't be it if you were stuck in
a telephone box.

Paul White, 8

Justin Barrett

Happy

Rudolph, Santa's reindeer is this when he eats all the carrots that people have left out for him before they go to bed.

Anne Christie, 9

You feel joyful, like if you've been tickled. It makes you jolly, you run around, laugh and do things.

Scott Price, 8

Budgies are this when they're singing, dolphins always seem to have a smile and hyenas are this when they're laughing. Mrs Thatcher would be this if she won the election next year and became Prime Minister again.

Laura Davidson, 9

Ross Hartshorn

Friend

You would need this person if you were in the jungle somewhere and you were just about to be eaten by a crocodile . . . you'd need him then, or her. Maybe if you were in a lot of trouble and you were wanted for something, you would need this person then, if ever you'd done something wrong and you wanted somebody to stick up for you, you'd need that person.

Donald Clark, 9

If somebody's bothering you, they'd go and tell them to stop bullying you – to pick on somebody your own size if you're quite small. If you're ill and that if there's this brilliant disco on that they wanted to go to, they'd miss an hour or half an hour of it to come and talk to you in case you're bored . . . and they'd bring something like chocolates or grapes.

Anne Christie, 9

Lucky

It's when you get a gift from God like being able to draw good or write good or have brains or something like that and when you get chosen for the netball team.

Beverley Williams, 8

In stories some people are very, very, very, very, very it.

Veronica Miller, 7

Surprise

When this happens to you, it happens suddenly, like
when you're walking downstairs something jumps
out of the stair cupboard and goes boo! and that has
done a certain thing to you, and that is what one of
those is.

Rupert Price, 9

If an extinct bird just suddenly showed up, it would
be this; if the studio suddenly blew up, it would be
this as well; if an aeroplane landed in your back
garden, it would probably be this as well; if you see a
shark with a machine gun in your custard, it would
be this as well.

Craig Bryce, 9

Simon Catley

Rainy Days

Bored

Scott Kelly

Boring

I think Jackanory on TV is this word and usually history in class is this word too. Polos can be very boring, too, and so can steak pie.

Justine McKellar, 9

Got nothing to do, it's raining, got nowhere to go, it's raining . . . I can't think of any more now.

Michael Simpson, 6

Sad

If a snail was unhappy it could sort of wriggle away and then go and find a place and curl up in its shell. If you had it for a pet, which would be a bit silly, and you didn't give it any food, it would be this word so it would maybe try and find its way out and go somewhere else.

Judith Ballantyne, 8

If my wee little sister got lost in the woods, my mother and father would be this word, and if one of the Queen's dogs got dognapped, she would be this word too.

Justine McKellar, 9

If you washed your dress in the sink without the bowl and you forget to pull it out when you pull the plug out . . . 'cause my grandma once. She putted her frock in there and that went down, it did, it went down the drain.

Marcus Stackermann, 5

Emma Spawton

Sulk

My friend in my class, she's a bit. Whenever she wins at parties she's all right, but when she doesn't win she goes all sulky and sulks. We went to this party and we had to pin the star on Wonder Woman's wand, and my friend got it instead of Anna – she didn't go sulky. It was all right after that. She doesn't do it that much now. She used to, though.

Lucy Cropper, 6

Say somebody tells you off for something you haven't done and you're really fed up about it and you go up to your bedroom and you sit down and you pull faces and that. You stay up there for about ten minutes or some people stay up there longer and you start shouting and screaming and that, and taking it out on other people and you're right miserable all that day.

Debbie Newburn, 11

Clumsy

There's a Mr Man called Mr . . . you know, and he is very it, you know, and he tears newspapers, gets marmalade on them, accidentally puts the cat in the bath instead of its basket . . . and he gets through several door knobs, so does Mr Strong.

Veronica Miller, 7

Worry

Grown-ups do it when they're out of money from the bank and when they've drawn too much they haven't got enough money left in, and when they've sort of run out of alcohol drinks they worry because they haven't got any money for any more.

Lyndon Nicholas, 10

Naughty

It's bad if you smash a window, if you knock on somebody's door and run away. If you throw your dad's camera down the stairs; if you don't behave yourself; if you're being bad.

Christopher Wishart, 8

It's when you've been naughty and you get smacked or something, and my friend, Jonathan, he's extremely, and sometimes I am a bit.

Lucy Fennings, 8

Rude

Annabel Sewell

Messy

It can be someone who like spills some jam all over them and slides in it. They can become this word, and sometimes when you get out of bed in the morning me hair's all over so it's this and if you like fall in some mud, your clothes become this, and like when you get up in the morning you can feel this sometimes unless you wear curlers or something to keep your hair in place.

Nicola Smith, 10

My brother is this word and he gets gravy on the tablecloth and sometimes little bits of potato, and when he eats rice he gets it sometimes on the floor.

Annelies Holiday, 5

Dianne Greenwood

Greedy

If you've been out to pick Christmas presents your mum says, 'What do you want?' and you pick all the dearest things. If you're looking through a catalogue and your mum says, 'I can't afford it,' and you say, 'Well, I don't care, I want it, she's got it why can't I get it, she always gets what she wants, I want what I want.'

Anne Christie, 9

You like food a lot, and if you like it so much you want to get more and more and more, and if someone else wants some you're always asking for theirs. You want more and more food and you can't stop eating.

Kimberley and Lee Kerrod, 8 and 11

Revenge

Samantha Mason

Angry

The Queen would be this if one of
her dogs did a toilet in the Palace.

Justine McKellar, 9

Gavin Seaton

Insult

Well, say someone is highly
intelligent and someone walks
along and says, 'Hello, dimwit',
that person would say, 'How dare
you insult me.'

Rupert Price, 9

It's when somebody calls you a stupid pig and you
don't like it and you really hate it and you start a fight
with them 'cause they've called you a right rude name
and you really hate it and you don't want them to call
you it again . . . so you beat them up.

Debbie Newburn, 11

Nag

Me sister is always the word to us if I won't dress her
doll or things like that . . . and sometimes me grandma
does the word to us when she wants to brush me hair
'cause she hurts, so that's why I don't like the word
when people do it to me, but sometimes I like doing it
to me little sister.

Nicola Smith, 9

Happy
Ever After

Love

You feel kind of shaky . . . you can feel silly if you kiss in the street or something when you're in this. You usually do things like kiss in the street that can make you very sort of embarrassed with all the people walking past looking at you. It's better to do it in the evening when there's hardly anybody about in the streets.

Ewan Jenkins, 10

When someone goes out with another person, and they have dates, and they keep going out together. And sometimes, if it goes too far, they get married.

Michelle Brown, 8

Amanda Westhead

Attractive

Well, it's someone really beautiful . . . they're usually
in television films, and they've usually had things
done to them, like had their teeth lifted.

Victoria Wilson, 9

It's when you're nice and you don't look like a pig or
a cow, and you right like people and you're not ugly
. . . you're just right nice and beautiful and everybody
likes you and you're right glamourous.

Debbie Newburn, 11

Well, something could be this if it were covered in
glitter or something, or all shiny . . . things that are
shiny like foil are this to crows, and they usually put
them in their nests.

Rupert Price, 9

Blush

I sometimes do it, but I don't any more . . . I'm not shy any more . . . I
used to do it when a friend came over and run upstairs and come down
when I felt like it but I don't any more. I've never seen adults do it but
they may do it when I don't see, when I'm out or something or when
I'm playing upstairs with my friends or something like that. They might
do it then but I've never seen them do it.

Sally-Ann Hardwidge, 6

Handsome

I think Paul Daniels is it
and the Blue Peter
people have to be it. Play
school people have to be
it. I don't think the
milkman is it at all.

Tom Groves, 7

Jonathan Meyers

Girlfriend

They come in all shapes and sizes. Sometimes, the
person is to your own taste. You like them very much
and to other people the person would be yuck!

Colin Armes, 10

Maybe you'd want one just to see
what it's like.

Ewan Jenkins, 10

My cousin's got one, and he don't
like her.

Paul White, 8

Boyfriend

It's the fashion to have one, and it's all the rage because they can be very attractive and it can make you popular with other people because they think you're really fantastic because you've got this beautiful person or thing with you and they really like you because of that, and they ask you how you managed to get this person.

Victoria Wilson, 9

I don't want one because they're pests . . . they ruin your life. They nose into everything you do and that, that's why I don't want one.

Tracey Stevenson, 9

You need one of these to get married. They could be useful if say you couldn't drive and they could – if you wanted to go out, they might be able to take you out. Some girls in our class have got one and some haven't, and I'm one of those that haven't.

Judith Ballantyne, 8

Little girls can not have them because they're too young but when you're about sixteen you can have one, and my sister's got one 'cause she's old enough, and I could only have one when I'm grown up because I'm too young just now. I might want one but I don't really know 'cause I might join the army when I grow up.

Lena Philpot, 7

Kerry Hale

Romance

It's when you fall in love, kiss, sleep together and get married, and live happy ever after. And you have a child and he grows up and he gets married, and he gets a child and that one gets a child, 'till the end.

Llewellyn Morgan, 8

Romantic

It's where two people go off together, and they have a good time and kiss and everything, and go into a room and switch the light off and start kissing and everything . . . and have a good time . . . and you have a good time and then you get married.

Stuart Butler, 9

Well it's like when you're in love with someone and sometimes the man takes you out to dinner in a quiet restaurant. Sometimes they don't – sometimes they go for a walk in the park, or walk along the seaside putting their arms around each other.

Leanne Collins, 7

Honeymoon

They go on islands and they get coconuts. They go round the world, and they might get a new car.

Phillip Wooderson, 6

If you have a really good one, it's when you don't argue with your wife or your husband.

Anne Christie, 9

If you had some children, you'd go without them, you'd just go by yourself.

Joseph Wallinger, 8

Teresa Jane Bland

List of Schools

Thanks are due to the following schools, and their pupils, for all their help and patience.

Abercrave Primary School Abercrave
Aloeric County Primary School Melksham
Archbishop Sumner School Streatham
Barham J & I School Wembley
Bellfield Community School Rochdale
Birtley East Primary School Birtley
Bishop Alexander Primary School
Newark on Trent
Bishopton J & I School Stratford upon Avon
Bolshaw Primary School Cheadle
Bromley School Pensnett
Cherry Orchard Primary School Worcester
Chorleywood Primary School Chorleywood
Church Road County Primary School Bolton
Chuter Ede Primary School Balderton
Cliffe Hill J & I School Halifax
Cranham Primary School Worcester
Cross Gates Primary School
Llandrindod Wells
Cyril Jackson School London
Damers County First School Dorchester
Drumgore Primary School Drumgore
Dunblane Primary School Dunblane
East Sheen Primary School East Sheen
Elgin East End School Elgin
Elgin West End School Elgin
Etherley Lane J & I School Bishop Auckland
Fairhaven School Wordsley
Fir Tree Primary School North Reddish
George Street Junior School Pontypool
Glashieburn School Aberdeen
Green Lane J & I School Middlesbrough
Harestanes Primary School Kirkintilloch
Heamoor County Primary School Penzance
Henknowle County Primary School
Bishop Auckland
Herne County Junior School Crowborough
Jarvis Brook County Primary School
Crowborough
Julian's Primary School Streatham
Kibblesworth Primary School Kibblesworth
Llandrindod Wells Primary School
Llandrindod Wells
Llanfair Caerfinion Primary School
Llanfair Caerfinion
Lochpots School Fraserburgh
Loirston School Aberdeen
Mawgan-in-Pydar County Primary School
St Mawgan
Meiford Primary School Meiford
Mount Hawke Primary School Porthtowan
Mount Pleasant School Brierley Hill

Ottery St Mary Primary School
Ottery St Mary
Parish C of E Primary School St Helens
Park Terrace J & I School Pontypool
Penrhos Primary School Penrhos
Queensdyke Primary School Witney
St Brendan's Primary School Craigavon
St Clare's Primary School Newry
St Columb Minor County Primary School
Newquay
St Flannan's Primary School Kirkintilloch
St John's Roman Catholic Primary School
Bromley Cross
St Mary's Episcopal School Dunblane
St Mary's Roman Catholic School
Dorchester
St Michael's C of E School Melksham
St Swithun's School Sandy
Sacred Heart Primary School St Helens
Sheen Mount Primary School Sheen
Southowram County Primary School
Halifax
South Park School Fraserburgh
South Queensferry Primary School
South Queensferry
Sparrow Hill Primary School Rochdale
Spaxton Primary School Spaxton
Stocksfield Avenue Primary School
Newcastle upon Tyne
Stogursey Primary School Stogursey
Stratford C of E J & I School
Stratford upon Avon
Streatham Wells School Streatham
Sunnyside Primary School Middlesbrough
Tenterden C of E Primary School
Tenterden
Tenterden County Infants School Tenterden
Tenterden St Michael's C of E School
Tenterden
The Ben Johnson Primary School London
Thomas Jolyffe J & I School
Stratford upon Avon
Tolcarne Junior School Newlyn
Towerhill Primary School Witney
Tregolls Primary School Truro
Trotts Hill Primary School Stevenage
Upper Caldecot Lower School Biggleswade
Wembley Manor School Wembley
West Hill Primary School Ottery St Mary
Windsor Hill Primary School Newry
Witney County Primary School Witney